Sydney Lever

Fireflies; Ballads and Verses

Sydney Lever

Fireflies; Ballads and Verses

ISBN/EAN: 9783742899590

Manufactured in Europe, USA, Canada, Australia, Japa

Cover: Foto ©ninafisch / pixelio.de

Manufactured and distributed by brebook publishing software (www.brebook.com)

Sydney Lever

Fireflies; Ballads and Verses

To the Memory

OF

CHARLES LEVER,

THE KINDEST OF FATHERS,
THE FIRMEST OF FRIENDS,
AND THE MOST GENIAL OF MEN,

THESE HUMBLE VERSES ARE

Reverently and Affectionately Dedicated,

BY HIS DAUGHTER,

SYDNEY LEVER.

775498

PREFACE.

IN offering this little collection of lyrics to the public in general, and musicians in particular, I take the liberty of stating here, that they were written chiefly, and almost solely, with a view to musical interpretation.

Having myself attempted composition, and knowing therefore the difficulties which beset the composer, I have endeavoured in the following verses to use the simplest words, and only those which are most *singable*, even at the expense of poetical form.

I take this occasion of thanking first: the Rev. Frederick Langbridge for my title, " Fireflies," which most aptly describes my work: a few transient flashes and darkness between! and also Messrs. Boosey & Co., Robert Cocks

& Co., T. B. Cramer & Co., and Stanley Lucas & Co., for their kind permission to reprint the following words, which have been set to music by the subjoined composers, and published by their respective firms, namely :—

Title.	Composer.	Publisher.
A Proposal (Duet)	Claude Trevor.	Stanley Lucas & Co.
The Brocade Gown.	Charles Marshall.	Robert Cocks & Co.
Love and Hope.	Claude Trevor.	Boosey & Co.
Mother's Advice.	Sydney Lever.	Robert Cocks & Co.
The Bell Founder's Song (under the Title of " 'Tis best ".	Charles Marshall.	Robert Cocks & Co.
The Wraith of a Song (Anima mia).	Charles Marshall.	T. B. Cramer & Co.
Angel's Visits.	Claude Trevor.	Robert Cocks & Co.
Joys that Fade.	Claude Trevor.	Robert Cocks & Co.

The two following part songs, viz. :—

Title.	Composer.	Publisher.
To Love and Friendship.	Claude Trevor.	Novello Ewer & Co.
Twilight.	Sydney Lever.	Novello Ewer & Co.

have been published with all copyrights reserved.

13 Upper Wimpole Street,
London, W., *August 31, 1883.*

CONTENTS.

	PAGE
AN APOLOGY,	1
LOVE AND HOPE,	3
THE STREAMLET,	6
FELICINA,	8
A PROPOSAL,	10
ANGELS' VISITS,	11
TWO'S COMPANY, THREE'S NONE,	13
ASSUNTA,	15
A VISION,	17
IN MAY-TIME,	18
THE GREAT ENIGMA,	20
A MAIDEN'S DOWER,	22
LOST LOVE,	24
THE BELL FOUNDER'S SONG,	26
MOTHER'S ADVICE,	28
LIFE'S STREAM,	31

CONTENTS.

A Problem,
Twilight,
The Ugly Duckling,
The Novice,
Neapolitan Boy's Song,
In Memoriam,
The Painter's Ideal,
In Doubt,
Too Late,
The Emigrant's Song,
The Two Sisters,
To Love and Friendship,
The Crystal Heart,
Midnight,
The Brocade Gown,
My Plot of Ground,
The Gallant Little Gunboat,
Welcome Home!
Joys that Fade,
True and Brave,
Maigloeckchen,
The Wraith of a Song,
The Three Suitors,
Peace of Soul,
Baby Hope,
Sainte Marie la Bonne,

CONTENTS.

	PAGE
SPRING AND AUTUMN,	92
DOST THOU REMEMBER?	94
LOYAL AND TRUE,	96
IN MAY,	98
LOVE AND TIME,	100
"SUUM CUIQUE,"	103
GATHERED!	106
THEY NEVER MET,	108
A LOVER'S GIFT,	110
MY WISH,	112
LIFE'S SHADOWS,	114
LOVE'S APPEAL,	116
LILLIE'S DREAM,	118
THE PENNY TOY VENDOR,	120
CHRISTMAS-TIDE,	123
CHRISTMAS HYMN,	125
NEW YEAR'S EVE	127
HARVEST HYMN,	129
HYMN,	132

FIREFLIES.

AN APOLOGY.

As lantern light is to the beacon's flame,
   So to poetic verse compares my rhyme,
The spark which kindles both is yet the same
   In every country and in every clime.

The poet, like the skylark, spreads the wing,
   And soars to worlds to other men unknown,
I, like the humble linnet, sit and sing
   My simple ditty for myself alone.

AN APOLOGY.

Yours is the organ, with its mighty chords
   Which set the breasts of half the world aglow,
I have my reed pipe, which perhaps affords
   As much of music as I e'er shall know.

Forgive me then, oh! ye of greater worth,
   I venture not to emulate your strain,
But I, too, love the beauties of this earth,
   And singing them find solace for my pain.

LOVE AND HOPE.

In the evening I sit in the twilight alone,
    As alone I must dwell evermore,
While I muse on the days and the joys that are gone,
    On the sorrows, perhaps, still in store.
Like the echo of wavelets that mournfully beat
    On a distant and desolate shore,
O'er my memory floweth the melody sweet
    Of a passionate love-song of yore.
      "O my sad heart, silence thy cry,
        Love must live on, tho' hope may die."

Oh! fair was my love in the days of its youth,
    Ere hope slowly faded away,
Oh! firm was my faith in his honour and truth,
    Whose love was as light to my day.
The shadows have fallen my spirit around,
    Night cometh and I might forget,
But e'en in my dreaming the sorrowful sound
    Of the tender refrain haunts me yet—

    "Oh! my sad heart, break with thy pain,
    Hope soon must die, tho' love remain."

    Hark, the sound of bells is stealing
        Thro' the shadows as they fall,
    And the chimes so sweetly pealing
        Unto rest and comfort call.
    O'er the hills and valleys bringing
        Solace to the soul in pain,
    Newer meaning seem they singing
        To the sorrowful refrain—

"Oh! my sad heart, tho' love may fail,
If faith endure, hope shall prevail."

THE STREAMLET.

Little Streamlet, bright and clear,
   What is this thy wavelets say,
Whispering softly in my ear
   As they speed upon their way?

"Glowing sunshine, darkening shade
   Flow'ring meadows, sombre wood,
Frowning rocks and smiling glade
   All alike are fair and good."

THE STREAMLET.

Little Streamlet, whence, I pray,
  This thy deep philosophy?
Would that I might learn to-day
  How to practise it from thee.

"Over pebbles—over sand
  Ever merrily I flow,
Spreading gladness through the land
  Singing softly as I go."

Little Streamlet, I would fain
  Learn the songs such joy that bring,
Sing, then sing them, once again
  That I too may learn to sing.

"'Neath the starlight and the dew,
  As beneath the summer air,
I my joyous course pursue,
  All is good and all is fair."

FELICINA, OR THE PAINTER'S MODEL.

Felicina is a picture
    In her brilliant-coloured gown,
And the crimson kerchief, binding
    Waving hair of darkest brown.

Felicina, like the swallows,
    Flits from south to north each year,
There, her life is full of gladness—
    Full of misery 'tis here.

FELICINA, OR THE PAINTER'S MODEL.

There, she straw-plaits in the sunshine
 Singing blithly as a bird—
Here, for hours she stands as model
 And her voice is never heard.

Patiently, without a murmur,
 Gains she thus her livelihood,
Growing every day more lovely,
 Every hour more pure and good.

Would that I were only wealthy,
 And could give her such a store,
As would take her back to Florence,
 Ne'er to wander any more.

A PROPOSAL.

"Prithee Maiden, shall I sing thee
Sweetest lays were ever known?"—
"No, no, not so,
I love nature's songs alone."

"Prithee Maiden, shall I bring thee
Jewels worthy of a queen?"—
"No, no, not so,
I love no gem ever seen."

"Prithee Maiden, may I fling thee
Down my heart, aye! at thy feet?"—
"No, no, not so.
Lest mine own in answer beat."

ANGELS' VISITS.

One autumn night when all was bare
I sat with my companion, Care,
I watched the leafless, waving trees,
And thought: My life is such as these.
She spoke no word but in her eyes
I read how rapidly Time flies,
How hollow is our longed-for fame—
How brief the glory of a name!
  I could not weep—I could not pray,
  My soul was weary of its day.

Anon amid the silent gloom
A sound of voices filled the room;
Care's form had faded, in her place
Stood figures of angelic grace
With folded wings and tender eyes,
And songs learnt far above the skies:
" Though pain and toil on Earth abound,
Above can truest joy be found ".
    My thirsty soul those words drank deep
    And I could pray—for I could weep.

TWO'S COMPANY—THREE'S NONE.

The porch outside the door,
   I'm sure you'll say with me,
Has room for two, for two, not more,
   Why are we ever three?

The settle by the stove
   Is only meant for two—
Then why does any one, my love,
   Sit there by me and you?

The grotto by the sea,
　　Where we have sat of yore,
Is wide enough for you and me,
　　But not for any more.

Why do not people know,
　　It is not hard to tell,
That what is charming, just for two
　　Won't suit for three as well.

ASSUNTA.

Assunta was her name, and she was fair,
    Although born under burning southern skies;
As golden threads gleamed all her silken hair,
    And Heaven seemed reflected in her eyes.

I, as an artist, prayed to sketch her face,
    (Of all my love—I know not if she knew)
She granted my request with quiet grace,
    Sat to me silent—silently withdrew.

I dar'd not speak, I held her far too dear
    To let her brave the subtle veilèd scorn
That she, my wife, would have encountered here
    When it was known that she was peasant-born

I left the place and wandered far away,
    To seek oblivion and pursue my art;
Assunta stayed at home to watch and pray
    And wait—until the waiting broke her heart.

A VISION.

I ponder'd o'er the Book of Life last night,
    While lost in reading, lo! I heard a sound,
I paused, and shading with my hand the light
    Rose from my seat and, wond'ring, gazed around.

Erect and still, behold! a figure stood
    In seraph wings and radiant robe of white,
And on its head it wore a golden hood,
    And held a silver lyre with gems bedight.

It spoke, its angel-eyes suffused with tears;
    "Cam'st thou to see a minstrel of the Lord?
Frail mortal, all the music of the spheres
    Should not have drawn thee from His precious Word!"

IN MAY-TIME.

When does the sun shine brighter
    All through the balmy day,
When does the heart feel lighter
    Than on a morn in May?
Then come the daisies gleaming
    Star-like the sward above,
To rustic girlhood seeming
    As oracles of love.
Then do the maidens shyly
    Test future fate by these,
While village swains are slyly
    Carving their names on trees.

The village swains are willing,
    But all the maids are coy,
With word and gesture chilling
    Each eager, pleading boy.
Till on one eve 'tis settled
    A childish game to try,
And now the swains are nettled,
    They vow "to do or die".
When sing the maids with laughter
    "Hold me who catch me can,"
The youths all running after,
    Secure a bride, each man.

THE GREAT ENIGMA.

How strange that men, whose end is in the grave,
   To which they nearer draw with every breath,
Should try to solve all matters, gay or grave,
   Yet scarcely give a passing thought to death !

Yet all who live must pass the sable door,
   The entrance to the terrible unknown,
Above whose arch are writ the words : " No More "—
   And pass it all unaided and alone !

THE GREAT ENIGMA.

And he, the Porter grim who keeps the gate,
    Whose veiled face we gaze on with affright—
Is he a fiend who mocks at mortal fate—
    Or Angel-Guardian of the Realms of Light?

Ah! fruitless questions flung to empty air!—
    Yet do they press upon us every day,
Symbol'd in all things budding fresh and fair,
    And fading slowly till they pass away.

To solve the great Enigma were a task
    Alas! for mortal intellect too high.
Beyond the portal death withdraws his mask,
    And men but learn the answer when they die.

A MAIDEN'S DOWER.

She was but a simple maiden
   When he sought her for his bride,
With no gifts or graces laden
   Love and Truth but nought beside,—
      Only these and nought beside.

Once in idle jest and chatter
   Did she fully joyous feel,
Now she loves the shuttle's clatter
   And the music of her wheel—
      Just the music of her wheel.

Now all fruitless pleasures leaving
   Sits she singing in her room,
Yards of home-spun linen weaving
   On her long-neglected loom—
      Her too long-neglected loom.

This alone shall be her dower
   Who has neither house nor lands,
Just the work which hour by hour
   Grows beneath her loving hands—
      Just the produce of her hands.

Still she labours at her spinning
   Rising early, working late—
Thus to prove, her heart in winning,
   Won he no unworthy mate—
      Won he no unworthy mate.

LOST LOVE.

Once with smile and joyful singing
    Would I meet thee at the gate;
Now with hands, impatient, wringing,
    Watch I all in vain, and wait.
Gone is from my voice the lightness
    Which could cause it's lays to flow—
Fled the golden dream whose brightness
    Made my heart with hope to glow.

      I love thee still, as in the days of yore,
      But thou, alas! thou lovest me no more.

LOST LOVE.

Would my breaking heart had power
    To disguise its bitter pain
If by that, for one brief hour,
    I might win thee back again.
But alas! 'tis not my failing
    Which has made thy heart grow cold;
Songs and smiles are unavailing
    To recall the love of old!

      I love thee still, as in the days of yore,
        But thou, alas! thou lovest me no more!

THE BELL FOUNDER'S SONG.

A Founder was making a little church bell
    And he sang to himself as he wrought,
And he worked at it cleverly—fashioned it well,
    Smiling sadly sometimes at his thought.

" 'Twill ring brightly and clear to the hearts that are light
    And sound sadly to those that have sorrow."
And he laboured away through the long winter's night
    For it had to be ready the morrow.—

" How short is the time here allotted, a span
    In which there's no leisure for breath—
And the three great events in the life of a man—
    Are his birth—and his marriage—and—Death.

" To think that the bell I am fashioning now
    With its merriest tinkle shall ring,
While the infant is crossed by the priest on the brow,
    And the Angels in Heaven shall sing!

" Then again for the bride in her gown of pure white
    On the brightest and happiest day
When two hearts that are faithful their loyalty plight
    While for them Guardian angels shall pray.

" And at last for the Soul which is freed from the load
    Of life's burden, and flees to its rest,
It shall sing to the mourners who tread the sad road :
    'Take ye heart, it is best, it is best'."

MOTHER'S ADVICE.

Last night when home was tidied up
    And all the work was done,
I thought I'd saunter out awhile
    To watch the setting sun.
For Robin often comes that way,
    Though always 'tis by chance,
And then he almost always
    Passes by with just a glance.
But yesternight he stopped and stay'd
    And then, after a while,
He begged I'd walk along the lane
    With him, just to the stile.

MOTHER'S ADVICE.

And mother says we girls were meant
   In all things to obey,
So when he bade me go with him
   How could I say him nay?

The lane is very short you know,
   Yet oh! 'twas such a while
Before we reached the end of it
   And rested at the stile.
And then he took my hand in his
   And begged me for a kiss—
You'll say you never heard before,
   Of daring such as this.
And yet 'twas done so modestly
   And in so sweet a way,
I could not find it in my heart
   To answer shortly, nay.
For men must be obeyed, and so—
   What could I do or say—

But tell him it was very wrong,
And let him have his way.

I know not half the words he said,
How many kisses stole,
I only know I pledged myself
To him with heart and soul.
And ne'er before in all my life,
Had moonlight shone so bright,
And mother says he's good and true,
And mother's always right.
Then when I said 'twas growing late,
I could not longer stay,
He answered, I should only go
When I had named the day.
And men must be obeyed, and so—
What could I do or say—
But tell him it was very wrong,
And let him have his way.

LIFE'S STREAM.

Too true it is that Life is like a stream
   On which must swim or sink each living soul.
Some with the current float and dream their dream,
   Others, against it, struggle to their goal.

The shallows are the little cares which make
   The total of our paltry human dole—
The whirlpools are the greater griefs that wake
   To strength or to despair the human soul.

The glowing flowers that grow on either bank
   Do but allure the heedless, idle hand—

LIFE'S STREAM.

All *they* have time to grasp are grasses rank
   Who strive, against the stream, toward the land.

Of those who sink we know not what may be,
   Enough to mark the many on their course;
The listless drifting to an Unknown Sea—
   The earnest seeking for the Unknown Source.

A PROBLEM.

I pray you, tell me what
   This mystery may be,
I understand it not,
   And oh! it troubles me.

When cousin Ralph is by,
   I hear my pulses beat,
And when he is not nigh,
   No joy in life is sweet.

A PROBLEM.

I feel the blushes rise
    The moment he appears,
And when he goes,—my eyes
    Are full of burning tears.

I have no word to say
    When out, alone, we walk,
Yet feel, when he's away
    For hours I could talk.

One name by night and day,
    I murmur scarce above
My breath, oh! pray you say,
    If this I feel be *Love?*

TWILIGHT.

Mark the shades of evening falling
    O'er the fields and meadows float,
Hark! the cuckoo sweet is calling
    Softly its familiar note.

Now the flowers are sweetly dreaming
    Of their days so bright, so few,
Soon the moonbeams silver streaming
    Will make diamonds of the dew.

All to rest and joy invite us
    After daylight's labour long,
Let then music's bond unite us
    To greet leisure with a song.

Life is short and half its pleasure
    Tends to sorrow while we taste
Of this brief—sweet hour of leisure,
    Let us then no moment waste.

They alone can best enjoy it,
    Who know long laborious days,
And no better can employ it
    Than in soft harmonious lays.

THE UGLY DUCKLING.

(AFTER ANDERSON).

A little ugly Duckling
    One day was hatched, I ween
No Duckling half so plain as this
    Had e'er before been seen.

Its beak was far too long,
    Its neck so wondrous fine,
Its mother muttered in amaze,
    " Can *that* be child of mine ? "

Her kinsfolk looked with scorn,
    Her neighbours shook their head,
She wept "Alas! that I was born,
    Oh! would that I were dead".

At last in her despair
    She placed her life at stake,
And spreading pinions on the air
    Flew swiftly o'er the lake

There 'mid a lordly throng,
    In plumage pale and wan
She found herself her kin among
    The Duckling was,—a *Swan*.

THE NOVICE.

The chants that filled the air
    Have died in silence now;
She kneels in silent prayer
    Who breathed but now her vow.
The incense-fumes like angel's wings
    Still hover o'er her head,
The lamps within their ruby rings
    A mellow radiance shed :
Before she seeks her convent cell
She kneels to bid the world farewell.

> "Farewell ye glades and meadows gay,
> Ye fields of waving golden corn,
> Farewell, ye blithesome birds whose lay
> Doth greet each crimson morn."

No care her heart invadeth,
  No doubts her senses blight,
All earthly glamour fadeth
  Before Religion's Light.
Her voice with holy fervour rings,
  Her eyes with rapture glow,
As with unfalt'ring lips she sings
  Farewell to all below.
The trial and the pain are past
And she has found True Peace at last.

> "Farewell thou smiling joyous earth,
> Farewell thou glad and glorious sun,
> A world of greater, richer worth
> My soul this day hath won."

NEAPOLITAN BOY'S SONG.

I am only a lad, and perhaps you will say,
    Such a boy can know nothing about it,
I maintain that to bask in the sunshine all day
    Is delight. Let them try it who doubt it.

And how do I manage for board and for bed?
    Why a piece of brown bread is my food, Sir,
And the steps with your hat folded under your head,
    Make a couch most uncommonly good, Sir,

Sometimes I am given a penny on trust
    By my neighbours who've jobs to be done, Sir,
For I'm able to work, and I do when I must
    But then go back and bask in the sun, Sir.

I am idle you say, but the adage knows best
    And lays down that all labour and strife, Sir,
But shortens our days—and so here let me rest
    In the sun for the whole of my life, Sir.

IN MEMORIAM.

In memory of me
    When I am gone,
Plant ye no cypress tree,
    Place ye no stone.

All that I ask or crave
    Is, that ye will
When I am in my grave
    Think of me still.

All that I wish to keep
    When I depart
Is just a corner, deep
    Down in your heart.

Where all my faults forgot,
    Only your love
Shall soar, oh! will it not?
    Failings above.

This be my monument,
    It is the best.
Say but "She came and went,
    God grant her rest".

A PAINTER'S IDEAL.

She is a maiden of high birth and stately,
    Would grace with her presence an Emperor's throne,
I am an artist, unknown until lately,
    And now, spite of effort, but partially known.

'Tis madness to love her! I know it is madness,
    But think you that lessens the sting or the pain?
And see here my pencil, in joy or in sadness,
    Has but reproduced the lov'd features again.

Mark, here, as Elaine in the mournful barge drifting
    Towards the sad sea—from which none may return,
And here as an angel, the censer uplifting,
    Where prayers of the faithful eternally burn.

Here again as a lady in powder and ruff,
    And that is a sketch as a fisherman's wife,
And that—nay, but surely 'tis more than enough,
    So close the portfolio,—and with it my life.

IN DOUBT.

The Spring was budding fresh and fair
 And all the earth was glad,
When in an arbour sat a pair,
 A maiden and a lad.

Of love and truth long spoke the youth
 She only laughed, and said :
" Perhaps upon Midsummer's Day
 I might consent to wed ".

But Summer came and Summer went,
   And still to all he said;
But an unwilling ear she lent,
   With an averted head.

"I cannot say—I cannot stay,
   For I must hurry home;
But if you like to ask, you may,
   When Michaelmas is come."

Then Autumn came and Michaelmas
   Had long been past and gone;
He pleaded still, and yet the lass
   Would give him answer none.

But with a sigh would hasten by
   To reach her cottage door,
Until he lost all hope, and vowed
   He'd never ask her more.

IN DOUBT.

But Christmas Eve (when none may grieve)
    Came round to make hearts glad;
And on the settle by the hearth
    They sat—that maid and lad.

To his surprise, with downcast eyes,
    She blushed exceeding red;
"If you should ask me once again
    I'll answer—'Yes,'" she said.

TOO LATE.

There was a time when you and I were young,
    When love was true, and we could smile at fate,
But those bright hours are now the past among
    And it is now—too late—too late!

Then came a time when mention of thy name
    Awoke my soul to passion 'kin to hate
And that too passed, and now I do not blame
    Nay, I forgive thee, but it is—too late!

Ask thou not then for what I cannot give.
    Deep is my calm, as once my love was great
So leave me now, content that I forgive
    My heart is dead—it is—too late—too late!

THE EMIGRANT'S SONG.

Away, far away o'er the surging Atlantic,
    With tearful eyes stung by the biting sea-foam,
Borne aloft and afar over billows gigantic,
    From country and friends, from dear Erin and home.

Take heart, boys, the Saints are still watching above us,
    The Mother of Mercies will hark to our call,
And the dear ones at home, in the old land who love us,
    Will pray that no evil our path may befall.

We'll work and we'll starve (if we must) but we'll save
    And hope to return to dear Erin once more,
So one cheer from your hearts in Farewell and be brave,
    Ere it pass from our sight, the bright Emerald shore.

What matters it, tho' we, her sons and her daughters,
    From homestead and country are ruthlessly cast,
And are sent to seek bread in a land beyond waters,
    So that God only bless our dear Erin at last!

THE TWO SISTERS.

"The man that I wed must have houses and lands
    Besides riches beyond all compare."

"With a poor man I loved, and who toiled with his hands
    For bare life, would I far sooner share."

"With jewels and gems too, my head he must crown
    Till the world should exclaim in amaze."

"I would far sooner shrink from all fame and renown
    So my loved one would glad me with praise."

"Apparelled in splendour, becoming my state,
    I would rule by a sign or a word."

"While I toiled in my cottage, both early and late
    Happy slave of my master and lord."

TO LOVE AND FRIENDSHIP.

WORDS FOR A PART SONG.

A toast to life's best joys
    Let's drink before we part,
Fill up your glasses, boys,
    And greet it from your heart.

First then to woman's love,
    A gem of peerless worth
All other gifts above
    Upon this gladsome earth.

We next to friendship's claim
    Your hearty greeting call,
That which endures the same
    Whatever fate befall.

TRIO:

Brief is our life and subject to much sorrow,
    Friendship and love alone can make it bright,
An honest grasp to wish us luck to-morrow,
    Tremulous lips to whisper low "Good Night".

A loving heart to share
    With us life's chequer'd road,
A friendly hand to bear
    A portion of its load.

A woman to adore,
    A man to hail as friend,
What can we wish for more
    Until we reach life's end?

Though youth and joy depart,
    Not lonely do we stand
While love links heart to heart,
    And friendship hand to hand.

THE CRYSTAL HEART.

A crystal heart with a silver rim
   Old-fashioned and quaintly chased
Engraved with a date grown faint and dim,
   And a monogram interlaced.

Oh! who can guess at the tale it told
   To her who first possessed it.
Oh! who can dream in the days of old
   How to breast and lips she pressed it.

In itself such a paltry and trifling thing
   Devoid of intrinsic worth,
Around it who knows what memories cling
   Of all that is purest on earth.

Alas! the crystal is crushed and riven
   Which of love long past was token.
Perhaps her heart to whom 'twas given—
   A richer gem—was broken!

MIDNIGHT.

Slumber sweet one while thou may'st
 Dreaming of a dawning bright;
All our dreams the fairest, gayest,
 Are but visions of a night.

Angels guard thy gentle slumbers
 Hov'ring softly o'er thy head,
While the stars in countless numbers
 Round thy couch their radiance shed.

MIDNIGHT.

Slumber on while dew-drops glisten
    On the Ivy round thy sill;
Dreaming on, forget to listen
    To my song, so soft and still.

Sweetest sounds alone should reach thee
    Through the region of thy dreams,
Not my words, lest they should teach thee
    Life is sadder than it seems.

Slumber on, nor ever hearken
    To my sorrow-sounding lay:
Never word of mine shall darken
    The bright dawning of thy day.

THE BROCADE GOWN.

In an attic where they gamboll'd
   Little cousins, he and she,
Stood an old oak chest o'er-shadowed
   By a withered Christmas tree.

Once when weary of their playing
   They had sat them down to rest,
She had told him in a whisper
   All the Legend of the Chest.

THE BROCADE GOWN.

'Neath that tree so lank and withered
   One who long years past was laid
Under sod, had stood and conquered
   In a gown of brown Brocade.

"In the year," so runs the Legend—
   Then triumphantly she cried :
"She who of my children's children
   Wears this gown shall be a bride".

Many maidens merely curious
   Oft the old Brocade had ey'd,
But the sleeves were so old-fashioned
   And the skirt so strangely wide.

Far he wandered, that dear cousin,
   Much the little maid did grieve—
Till at last came joyful tidings
   He'd returned on Christmas Eve.

Taking heart, the little maiden,
    Half triumphant, half afraid;
Musing on the olden Legend
    In that gown herself arrayed.

And she waited in the attic
    Where of old they oft had played
Till he came to find his playmate
    In the gown of brown Brocade.

Need I say ere Autumn faded
    Into Winter stern and cold
They were wed, the former playmates,
    As the Legend had foretold.

MY PLOT OF GROUND.

(AN ALLEGORY).

I had a little plot of ground
   Claim'd from a neighbouring field
I made a paling all around,
   And in the grass concealed
The violets began to blow,
And modestly their heads to show.

It was a modest little spot.
　　The owner of the field
Laughed at my work, forbade me not,
　　And hoped that it would yield
"Much produce to the industrious care
That for it—did no trouble spare".

"Ah! Sir," I shyly made reply,
　　"I do not wish from it
Aught, but its tribute to the sky
　　It bore—when first I lit
Upon it, in the meadow's border,
And trimmed and set it into order."

An' so it yield you pleasure may
　　Keep this ground for your own,
You ne'er shall hear me say you nay,

MY PLOT OF GROUND.

Nor ask you what you've sown."
And then he laughed and went his way,
Ah! that was such a happy day!

But ah! the reapers came to reap,
   And up my flowers tore;
In vain did I appeal and weep,
   They only laughed the more!
" What, call you that a garden, child?
'Tis full of weeds all rank and wild!"

" But if the weeds are dear to me,
   I love them dearly, dearly!"
" What would the master say to thee?
   What do you pay him yearly?"
" He saw, and never said me 'nay,'
He only laughed, and went his way."

But then the mowers came to mow.
And mow'd away my flowers!
I saw, yet never dared say '*no*,'
The work of happy hours!
And when all trace away was swept,
I sat me down alone and wept.

THE GALLANT LITTLE GUNBOAT.

(AN EPISODE OF THE BOMBARDMENT OF ALEXANDRIA).

Our captain piped all hands on deck,
    And said to all on board,
" My orders are to wait afar,
    Unless a chance afford ".

We murmured at the hard decree,
    " We might have stay'd at home,"
He answered lightly, " Trust to me,
    The chance shall *surely* come ".

Cheer, boys—cheer,
Ere o'er those forts so wooing
The rising sun appear,
We shall be up and doing.

Next day in silence stern and grim,
He overhaul'd each dirk,
'Twas hard on us—but more on him,
To have no room for work.

At last he cried, "Now, clear the decks,
Each man stand by his gun,
We've got the chance—now then for Mex:
Up steam—and let her run".

Cheer, boys—cheer,
Before the setting sun
Again shall disappear,
There's glory to be won.

THE GALLANT LITTLE GUNBOAT.

Then—Well done ! Condor—shot aloft,
   In bunting bright and gay,
Our gallant Captain and his crew
   Had fought and won the day.

And when we joined the fleet again,
   As night was falling fast,
You should have heard the ringing cheer
   They gave us, as we passed.

      Cheer, boys—cheer,
   When it is worth th' endeavour,
   Let those who like it, jeer,
   We are just as good as ever.

WELCOME HOME!

With steady heads and hands,
    And faithful hearts, I ween,
They went to serve, in foreign lands,
    Our country and our Queen.
The stoutest hearts may quail
    When parting time draws near,
When heroes' cheeks grow wan and pale
    For sorrow, not for fear.

WELCOME HOME!

Yet hip, hip, hip, hurrah,
   Rang out along the line,
  Drowning the sound of fife and drum,
   And tune of "Auld Lang Syne".

'Neath Egypt's burning sun,
   Not counting gain or cost,
With many a battle hardly won
   And many a brother lost;
They fought as brave men can
   And vied to bear the brunt
Of battle, every single man
   With fame or death in front.

Still hip, hip, hip, hurrah,
   Rang out throughout the fight,
  And cheering still, though wearied out
   They sank to rest at night.

But now the din of battle
    And all its horrors o'er;
Still is the Gattling's rattle,
    Silent the cannon's roar;
Now worn with want and toil,
    And longing but for rest.
How shall our native island soil
    Her sons give greeting best?

    With hip, hip, hip, hurrah,
        And welcome home once more
    Our men and lads are brave and bold.
        As ever were of yore!

JOYS THAT FADE.

The Spring was budding bright,
    The bells were ringing gay,
To herald in the light
    Of the first dawn of May.
My heart was free,
    My heart was young,
My voice could echo
    All they rung.

JOYS THAT FADE.

The bells rang sweet, the bells rang low,
    Within the belfry high,
And seemed to tell of joy below,
    And blessing in the sky.

But soon cold Autumn's shade
    Fell over flow'r and field—
Type of the joys that fade!
    Type of the hearts that yield!
My heart is sad,
    My heart is cold,
I cannot listen
    As of old.

The bells ring still o'er vale and hill
    Their soft and soothing lay,
But to my heart so dead and chill,
    It is no longer May!

TRUE AND BRAVE.

Once before an ancient mirror
    Stood a lassie and a lad;
Of the twain reflected in it,
    One was gay—the other, sad.
She had never tasted sorrow—
    Never dreamt of love or pain;
He was leaving on the morrow,
    When, ah! when to come again!

"See," he sighed, "our fortunes differ
    As our faces differ there!
I am poor, alone, and friendless,
    You are happy, rich, and fair!"

Years had passed, and Fortune changing,
    Robbed of wealth the little maid:
Changed in heart, without a murmur
    All her state aside she laid.
Tending sheep throughout the day-time,
    When the shades of evening fell
She would go to fetch the water
    From the limpid forest well.
Once upon its tranquil surface
    She beheld (as once of yore)
A familiar face beside her
    Only—nearer than before!

"Tried and True," the neighbours called her,
    And they dubbed him "Brave and Bold,"

And the church, when they were wedded,
    Scarcely half their friends could hold!
And so long did toast and cheering
    And congratulations last,
That their steps when homeward wending
    Saw the day declining fast.
And their shadows lay before them
    'Neath the golden setting sun,
Not as once, apart and lonely,
    But now blended into *one*.

MAIGLOECKCHEN.

(LILIES OF THE VALLEY.)

In Germany there is a tale
 Full often told and sung,
That Lilies of the Valley, pale,
 Are bells, by angels rung.

Their little bells, each coming spring
 Of each returning year
Do welcome, with a joyous ring
 We, mortals, cannot hear.

But we, if pure we live and die,
 In our allotted time
Shall learn their language in the sky
 And hear their merry chime.

THE WRAITH OF A SONG.

(ANIMA MIA.)

Long years ago 'neath Italy's blue sky
    I heard a song which I shall ne'er forget
Its every stanza ended in a sigh
    As of a soul whose sun of life had set.

    * " Anima mia, non ti ricordi più
        Di quel amor, di quel amor che fù ? "

    * ("Oh ! my beloved, hast thou not e'en a sigh
        For our dear love, the love of days gone by ? ")

The evening breezes, as they pass me by,—
    The sun-lit wavelets of the rippled lake—
All ask the question which knows no reply,
    And keep remembrance in my soul awake.

    "Anima mia, non ti ricordi più
        Di quel amor, di quel amor che fù?"

Ah! plaintive burden of a broken heart,
    Whose wail still sounds across a waste of years,
The very phantom of a song thou art
    Whose essence vanished long ago in tears.

    "Anima mia, non ti ricordi più
        Di quel amor, di quel amor che fù?"

THE THREE SUITORS.

A lovely maid of high degree
    Within a castle dwelt,
And at her feet young lovers three
    In deepest homage knelt.

The first, a prince full brave and bold,
    Did plead without avail,
She said: "I will not share your gold
    For earthly riches fail".

The next, a knight in armour deck'd,
   Did offer might and fame;
"Fair homes," she said, "your sword has wreck'd—
   I will not bear your name."

The last, a minstrel poorly clad,
   Approached with humble grace,
His song of love was low and sad,
   But hope shone in his face.

"No lands, no fame, no worth have I,"
   He sang with bated breath,
"But for thy sake I'd gladly die
   And bless thy name in death."

"Then live," she cried, "and be my lord
   For, by the stars above,
I value neither crown nor sword,
   But dearly hold thy love."

PEACE OF SOUL.

My life is like a ship at sea
   By tempest overtaken,
By Heaven doomed a wreck to be,
   By human hands forsaken.
Let thunder roar and breakers roll
So peace, sweet peace possess my soul.

Time was when, with a fearless eye,
   I gazed without emotion

PEACE OF SOUL.

On time, as years went passing by
    Upon life's fitful ocean,
And yearned to brave both reef and shoal
With peace, sweet peace within my soul.

But now that life has nought to give,
    The stormy billows cresting
My little bark still strives to live
    The gale and breakers breasting,
That it may reach it's hallowed goal
With peace, true peace within my soul.

BABY HOPE.

I've heard of fair young mothers who had lost
    Their one sweet pledge of love—their only child,
Yet bravely strove to hide the pain it cost
    Their loving hearts, before their lords and smil'd
Lest it should grieve the father more to mark
    Their grief—they tearless bore the weary day,
Content if they could snatch when it grew dark
    An hour, beside their baby's grave to pray!

And in my soul I bore a spirit child,
  A baby Hope—and rocked it in my arms.
Its father came and looked at us and smil'd,
  That I could ne'er grow weary of its charms!
But ah! my baby died, and in the grave
  I, tearless, laid its little drooping head,
And for his sake—the father's—I am brave,
  And none but he and I know Hope is dead.

SAINTE MARIE LA BONNE.

Fronting low and level sands,
    Backed by hills of olive wood,
Lo! a little chapel stands
    Raised to Ste. Marie the Good.
There the maidens stop to pray
    As they trip along the sands;
There the seamen, as they stray,
    Cross their brows with horny hands.

When the waves beat loud and wild
   On that little white-washed wall,
Wife and widow, maid and child,
   Loud on Heaven's mercy call.
Crouching at the grated door,
   Clinging to the lattice high,
Up to God their pleadings soar
   Through the dark and stormy sky.

Once when weary of the strife
   Raging in this soul of mine
Through a long and lonely life,
   Paused I at that humble shrine;
And I know not whence or why
   Came that sudden heart-felt throb,
But my prayer was but a sigh,
   And my pleading but a sob.

*   *   *   *   *   *   *

Once again before I die
    Doth my spirit long to be
'Neath that sad Italian sky,
    Near that lapping southern sea:
Murmuring the words divine
    Which my soul first understood,
Kneeling at the lowly shrine
    Of sweet Ste. Marie the Good.

SPRING AND AUTUMN.

Fair Spring in its luxuriant verdure clad
    To youth and freshness may new treasures bring
Of hope and joy—but oh! the hearts are glad
    Already, which feel lighter in the Spring.
To those whose souls are weary in Life's ways
    The drowsy calmness of the scented air,
The deep blue skies and cloudless, sun-lit days
    Speak not of Hope, but rather of Despair.

SPRING AND AUTUMN.

Those who have suffered aye love Autumn best ;
    The fallen leaves make music in their ears—
The pale blue Heavens breathe an endless rest,
    And fresh keen breezes dry unbidden tears.
Sweet Autumn with its tints of brown and gold,
    And scents of earth and grass late steeped in rain,
Speaks sympathy to hearts untimely old
    And soothes, because it understands their pain.

DOST THOU REMEMBER.

Dost thou remember how in childhood's hours
    I used to climb the rugged dizzy height,
To fetch thee ferns and blossoms, that the flowers
    Might weave a crown to deck thy tresses bright?

Dost thou remember how in later days,
    Beneath the silver moon's transparent beam,
Thy voice would sing the soothing southern lays
    While I would listen almost in a dream?

Dost thou remember how in later years,
    When loss and sorrow came on me apace,
Like balmy dew fell on my soul thy tears
    And as the sunshine cheered thy smiling face?

And now, and now, despite the flight of time!
    The roar and turmoil of the world above,
Our hearts still ring their sweet harmonious chime
    And sound the hours but as they're struck by love.

When youth, and hope, and joyfulness decline,
    And seem but as a lovely story told,
Sit by me, love, with thy dear hand in mine
    And I shall be as happy as of old.

LOYAL AND TRUE.

Sweet summer silence everywhere
    Hung over vale and hill,—
As tho' the tender peace to share
    The very birds were still,
And all around, the earth and sky,
    Seem'd loth the spell to break,
As he and I—my love and I—
    Our solemn pledges spake.

LOYAL AND TRUE.

"Loyal and True, Love, from to-day—
    Loyal and true, happen what may,
Loyal and true, Love, from to-day—
    Loyal and true, ever and aye."

Now winter's garment everywhere
    Lies soft, and white, and chill,
And mirror'd are the branches bare
    Upon the frozen rill.
My Love and I are far apart,
    Yet scarce is absence pain,
For still my heart—my loving heart—
    Re-echoes the refrain :
"Loyal and true, as on that day—
    Loyal and true, tho' far away—
Loyal and true, as on that day
    Loyal and true, ever and aye !"

IN MAY.

We wander'd through the fields in May—
The flow'rs were smiling, sweet and gay—
Our hearts were young and fresh as they;—
      No sorrow yet had we.

The birds sang gaily overhead,
The grass bent softly 'neath our tread,
The brooklet sparkling by us sped
      On, on toward the sea!

IN MAY.

We spoke of days and joys to come,
We planned our little cottage home
Midst fields wherein we were to roam
   In May-time, he and I !

But Autumn came and coldly sighed
And shed its sad leaves seared and dried—
And oh ! my darling drooped and died
   As flowers droop and die !

The fields will bloom again in May,
The birds will sing their thrilling lay,
The brooklet murmur on its way
   On, on towards the sea.

Alone I wander by the shore
And listen to the ocean's roar,
And ask the sad waves o'er and o'er :
   " Where shall our meeting be ? "

LOVE AND TIME.

(A LEGEND).

One day, when Time with weary feet
Was treading his accustomed beat
    Along the vale of Years,
He met young Cupid, erst so glad,
But now, alas! a sorry lad—
    All bathed in burning tears.

His broken bow lay by his side :
"Alas ! alas !" the youngster cried,
    "For Love is growing cold,
And maids won't wed, and men won't woo,
And Cupid has no work to do,
    As in the days of old !

"Then, lads and lassies owned my might,
And people fell in love at sight,
    Nor faltered on the brink !—
But *now*, rebellious to my sway,
They hesitate upon the way,
    And even pause to think !"

"Take heart," said Time, "and mend thy bow,
For hearts again will tender grow
    In every land and clime,

And wonders in thy quiver lurk,
If but to aid thee in thy work
    Thou'lt take the help of Time."

"SUUM CUIQUE."

(WRITTEN AND SENT WITH A SIGNET RING BEARING THE ABOVE MOTTO.)

"To every one his own"—nor less, nor more—
This the bold motto that, in days of yore,
Thy mailèd sires on their pennon bore:
    "To every one his own".

"To every one his own"—to all, fair play—
I would not wish to stand in others' way,
But let them see how 'cross my path they stray—
    "To every one his own".

"To every one his own."—I would redress
The wrongs of e'en a foeman in distress;
I claim my rights, nor would accord him less:
"To every one his own".

"To every one his own."—Fearless and bold
The woman's love which does to mine unfold
With my own life will I defend and hold:
"To every one his own".

"To every one his own."—Let no man dare
The friendship of my chosen friend to share—
It is a treasure far too rich to spare.
"To every one his own".

"To every one his own."—Let Fortune frown—
I grudge not any man his laurel crown,
To each would I award his due renown—
"To every one his own".

SUUM CUIQUE.

"To every one his own."—Whate'er men's creeds—
I reverence them for their lives and deeds—
For many a path to the great Portal leads:
    " To every one his own ".

"To every one his own."—Whate'er befall,
Be this life's joys and sorrows great or small,
'Tis Heaven awards them and dispenses all:
    " To every one his own ".

GATHERED!

(SUGGESTED BY A PICTURE BY MRS. LAWSON.)

 Gathered roses, fainting, dying,
  Laid together in a heap,
 Listen to their silent crying,
  Watch them as they tearless weep!
 Ah! those tender stems so broken,
  And those leaves that fade and fall,
 Are they not a fitting token
  Of a love beyond recall?

GATHERED!

Once with freshness were they gleaming,
    Those sweet petals now so pale,
Type of love, whose tender dreaming
    Wakes to falter and to fail.
Like the ruthless hand that scatters
    Richest roses on the soil,
Fate too, gathers up and shatters
    Love, the prize for which we toil.

Yet as roses leave their semblance
    In the perfume of their leaves,
So doth love live in remembrance
    In the constant heart that grieves.
So we gather up each token,
    Leaf of ruby and of gold,
Symbols of a love unspoken,
    And of constancy untold.

THEY NEVER MET.

(WRITTEN TO THE REV. F. L., POET AND PASTOR.)

Who says that men and women rue
A friendship, which must breed regret?
I know a couple—tho' 'tis true—
    They never met.

They each to each their choicest give,
The book he wrote, the song she set;
In perfect harmony they live. . . .
    They never met.

THEY NEVER MET.

Upon his poetry she dotes
(She's not too old for verses yet)
He writes the daintiest of notes—
    They never met.

They have no hardships and no wrongs—
No hasty language to forget;—
She loves his books, he likes her songs—
    They never met.

No dream of broken vows and heart
Has made them wake with eyelids wet,
They know not what it is to part—
    They never met.

I will not try nor can I dare
A moral out of this to get;
I say there is of friends a pair—
    Who never met.

A LOVER'S GIFT.

A little rose tree on a window sill
   In a China-jar—blue and white—
By a maiden, loving, (as maidens will)
For the sake of the giver, was tended still
   At morning, and noon, and night.

She watched each bud with the tenderest care,
   Ever longing for one to blow,
For had he not said that she must look, there,
In the heart of the flower, most fresh and fair,
   His unwavering faith to know.

But each morning a bud all withered she found,
  Till at last—only one still grew,
And this which her hopes had still flitted around
Blossom'd only to shed its pale leaves on the ground—
  And she felt that her Love was untrue.

MY WISH.

Brightly shines the sunlight, glowing
    Rosy red o'er flower and field,
Smiling upon all, bestowing
    Kisses on the half concealed
Violets blue—who lowly growing,
    Sweetest perfume yield.

Sweetest sounds the rills are singing,
    Winding thro' the lordly wood,
Ivy green to old oaks clinging,
    Seems in tender playful mood,
And the bells are gaily ringing,
    Truly all is fair and good.

MY WISH.

Oh! had I but fairy power
    For a space o'er thee and me,
Soon I'd change with that blue flower
    Or the ivy would I be.
Thou, the sunlight for an hour
    Or the stately old oak tree!

LIFE'S SHADOWS.

There are days on which the sunshine
   Seems to struggle with the rain,
There are faces which, when smiling,
   Seem to bear the mark of pain.

Days like these can ne'er be joyous,
   Yet they have a chastened grace—
Like the gentle tender smiling
   Of a sorrow-furrowed face.

LIFE'S SHADOWS.

As the showers to the blossom
    Which they nourish thus on earth,
Even so the tears of sorrow
    Nourish souls to greater worth.

As the sunshine seems more mellow
    For the shadows lately cast,
So the smiles on faces weary
    Seem to gild the trials past.

Light and laughter best are suited
    For the threshold of this life.
Chastened smiles and chequered sunshine
    For the souls who've borne the strife.

LOVE'S APPEAL.

Radiant daughter of the South,
 What a wealth of love there lies
On that coral-tinted mouth,
 In those dark and pensive eyes!

'Neath that breast like mountain snow
 Gilded by the setting sun,
Beats a heart whose fervent glow
 Waits but to be woke and won.

LOVE'S APPEAL.

Would that I might dare express
    Half what rushes to my lips,
Would that I might only press
    Silently thy finger tips.

Art thou cold or only proud,
    Whence this calm of thine so deep?
While my heart beats fast and loud,
    Must I ever silent keep?

Speak, if but to bid me go,
    Should my presence give you pain,
Speak, if but to answer no,
    If my cherished hopes are vain.

Stately is thy queenly gait,
    Evenly thy pulses beat,
Must I ever silent wait,
    Kneeling hopeless at thy feet?

LILLIE'S DREAM.

A maiden sat lonely one sweet summer's day,
    And wistfully gazed towards the west,
Then her eyes closed, and lo! she seemed wafted away
    To the side of her dearest and best,

For she dreamed that the distance was only a dream,
    And that e'en as she slept, he was near,
So life-like his clasp of her hand, did it seem,
    And so real his voice in her ear.

"Oh wake, sweetheart, wake, I've returned to the shore
　Of my dear native land, and to you,
To quit it, and thee, nevermore, nevermore."
　And she woke, and behold! it was true.

THE PENNY TOY VENDOR.

"Oh! Sirs, I am hungry and wretchedly clad,"
   She murmured, along the cold street.
"If not for my sake, for the sake of the lad
   Who doth cling to my lingering feet.

"See my little son here, he's but seven years old
   Yet he's walked all the day, with no cry,
Tho' he's hungry and weary, and oh! so cold,
   Of your mercy—good gentlemen, buy.

"See here is a pair of small dolls for a penny,
    And here is a tumbler in red,
For the love of the Lord take but one, and take any,
    But let us have means to get bread."

And this was the strain of her sorrowful song,
    As she wandered about hour by hour,
The thickly-thronged streets of the city along
    Through the gale, and the snowstorm, and shower.

"Oh! mother, you're weary," now spoke the young child,
    "For fainter is growing your cry,
'Tis I who will bid them," he said, and he smil'd
    And then cried "Come and buy, come and buy.

"I am sturdy and strong and but seven years old,
    I'm for sale for a penny," he said,
"For my mother is dying of hunger and cold—
    Oh! but save her, before she is dead."

Then a woman, or Angel—alas! who shall tell,
　Her face was so pure and so mild—
Whispered: "Let me take charge of thy mother, as well
　As of thee, my brave, strong-hearted child."

CHRISTMAS-TIDE.

Christmas is not always merry
   When our childhood's years are past,
Laurel-bush and holly-berry
   Mournful shadows often cast.

Thoughts of those on whom we squandered
   All our hearts held highest, best—
Thoughts of those who far have wandered,
   And of those who are at rest!

These are they which mar our gladness,
    Crowding in upon the brain;
Yet doth hope amid our sadness,
    Whisper: Ye shall meet again.

Meanwhile, all around, the living
    Claim our kindness and our care,
There is still the *joy of giving*
    Which God grants us as our share.

If but *one* sad heart we lighten—
    If but *one* sad life we cheer—
If *one* lot we help to brighten—
    Taste we not of Heaven here?

One such crumb of comfort, casting
    On Life's Ocean weird and wide,
Shall we find a joy more lasting
    Than a merry " Christmas-tide ".

CHRISTMAS HYMN.

He came, the Lord expected long,
To shield the weak, restrain the strong,
Commend the right, rebuke the wrong,
    Alleluia!

He came to rid the world of taint,
To help the sinner, bless the saint,
And cheer the heart with sorrow faint,
    Alleluia!

CHRISTMAS HYMN.

He came, our Pattern and our Guide,
To bid us lay all sin aside,
And spread salvation far and wide,
Alleluia !

Whene'er we celebrate His Birth,
Oh ! may we strew His gifts on Earth,
And strive for lives of greater worth,
Alleluia !

Ye faithful who His temple throng,
Oh ! be your Anthems loud and long,
Ye echo but the Angels' song :
Alleluia !   Amen.

NEW YEAR'S EVE.

The solemn night was dark,
   Yet balmy as in May,
As, loth to part—with heavy heart,
   The old year went his way.

I set the casement wide,
   And on the darkling night
Each smile and tear of the past year
   Rose pictured to my sight.

And every now and then
    From roof and porch would fall
A drop of rain—as tho' in pain
    For time beyond recall.

"Old Year," I whispered, "stay,
    I'll bear with every pain,
If thou the joy without alloy,
    Wilt bring me back again."

My face was wet with rain,
    While from the swaying trees
For all reply—a long-drawn sigh
    Seemed borne upon the breeze.

New Years may come and go,
    New hopes may rise and set,
But oh! the past will o'er them cast
    The shadow of regret!

HARVEST HYMN.

Thou, whose bounteous mighty hand
Scatters plenty o'er the land,
Or withholds it for a space
But to grant some greater grace :
Hear us, as we sing and pray
Thankfully to Thee to-day,
And our hearts and voices raise
To Thy everlasting praise.

HARVEST HYMN.

Thee we thank for garnered wheat
And for meadows fresh and sweet,
Thee, for gathered wine and oil
Borne on this or other soil.
Let all hands and tongues rejoice,
Praising Thee with but one voice,
Be the harvest great or small
'Tis Thy power ruleth all.

Thou who dost the sparrows feed
Wilt not fail us in our need.
Thou, for whom the lilies grow,
Well our many needs dost know.
While we still on earth must live,
Day by day sufficient give,
And, for strength to meet the strife
Grant, oh grant the Bread of Life.

Hearken to our falt'ring song

Joining in creation's throng,

Praising Thee with Heaven's Host

Father, Son, and Holy Ghost.

HYMN.

Be Thou my Guide, O Lord—be Thou my Guide
    Along the thorny path of Life's rough way,
I dread its terrors and would step aside,
    Hold Thou my hand, lest I should go astray.

Be Thou my strength, O Lord—be Thou my strength,
    In all this pain, my comfort and my stay!
Thus as each hour drags out its weary length
    My courage shall be even as my day.

HYMN.

Be Thou my Light, O Lord—be Thou my Light,
   Shine in my soul, distraught with darkling fears,
Dispel the terrors of this world's dark night,
   And let me see Heaven's dawning thro' my tears.

Be Thou my Friend—I have no friend but Thee,
   In Thy great mercy pardon all the past,
Sustain me now and in Eternity,
   Let me find rest, O Saviour, *rest* at last.

THE END.

www.ingramcontent.com/pod-product-compliance
Lightning Source LLC
Chambersburg PA
CBHW020057170426
43199CB00009B/312